Stephen R. Riggs

Protestant missions in the northwest

Stephen R. Riggs

Protestant missions in the northwest

ISBN/EAN: 9783743333741

Manufactured in Europe, USA, Canada, Australia, Japa

Cover: Foto ©ninafisch / pixelio.de

Manufactured and distributed by brebook publishing software
(www.brebook.com)

Stephen R. Riggs

Protestant missions in the northwest

PROTESTANT MISSIONS

In The Northwest,

BY

REV. STEPHEN R. RIGGS, D. D.

ACKNOWLEDGMENTS.

The writer of this paper has gathered the facts in regard to the Mission of the American Board of Commissioners for Foreign Missions, among the Ojibwas, from the Missionary Herald mainly, having received some suggestions from Mrs. Leonard H. Wheeler. The materials for the history of the American Board's work among the Sioux have been within my own knowledge.

For the short account of the Swiss Mission I am indebted, mainly, to Rev. S. W. Pond.

Dr. Alfred Brunson, in the "Western Pioneer," and Judge Gale's "Upper Mississippi," have furnished the materials for the Methodist Episcopal Mission among the Sioux and Ojibwas.

For the account of the work of the American Missionary Association among the Ojibwas, I am indebted to Dr. Strieby and Mr. S. G. Wright.

And lastly, I am quite obliged to Bishop H. B. Whipple for the communications of Rev. E. S. Peake and himself. This brief history of the Missions of the Protestant Episcopal Church among the Ojibwas and Sioux, is mainly in the form which they furnished.   S. R. RIGGS.

BELOIT, WIS., May, 1880.

If the question be asked, why, in the first settlement of this country, Protestant Missions were not pushed westward among the Aborigines, as Catholic Missions were, the answer is two-fold. First.—The pilgrims of New England came for the purpose of making homes, with freedom to worship God, for themselves and their children. Trading with the Indians appears to have been an after-thought, and efforts to convert them to the religion of Christ were left to be made by individuals, as they were moved by the Holy Ghost. On the other hand, the first immigrants to Nouvelle France, came for the purposes of trade, and Catholic Missions were believed to be necessary helpers in the fur-trade. Thus the influence of the government of France, and of its colony, was given to the extension of the Roman Catholic religion.

Second.—The traders of New France found themselves located on the water that flowed from the great lakes. These formed a natural and convenient high-way, for both trader and priest, to visit the Hurons, Ottowas and the Illinois tribes. Hence we find them, more than two centuries ago, on Lake Huron, and at the head of the Gitche Gumme or Lake Superior, and on Lake Michigan, and even down the Illinois river.

In the meantime, while the Protestants, hemmed in by the mountains, were making homes on the Atlantic coast, John Eliot, the Mayhews and David Brainerd, among the Mohegans and Delawares, were as zealous and successful in converting Indians to christianity, as any of the Jesuit Fathers among the Hurons. And a century afterwards, before the emigration of white people had crossed the Alleghanies, the Moravian missionaries followed the Delawares into western Pennsylvania and Ohio, and their labors were crowned with success.

But this far northwest was, until after the beginning of the present century, almost an unknown country to the Protestant communities of the United States. As the settlements came westward, the Christian churches were too much engaged in "strengthening their stakes" to do much at "lengthening their cords."

After the American Fur Company had made Mackinaw their depot of supplies for the northwest, Rev. William M. Ferry, a graduate of Union College, and father of the present Senator Ferry, of Michigan, in 1822, came to explore the field, and in the following year, with his wife, commenced the Mackinaw school, where, for many years, were gathered Indian children from all the tribes in this northwest territory. This may be our starting point; for quite a number of the half-bloods, children of traders and others on the upper Mississippi and Minnesota, were afterwards found to have been scholars in this school.

SECTION I.

MISSION OF THE A. B. C. F. M. WITH THE OJIBWAS, 1830.

The Ojibwas, or Chippewas as the name was formerly written, belong to the Algonkin family. Two hundred years ago they appear to have been occupying only the shores of Lake Superior and farther east. But coming first into contact with white people, and obtaining from them fire arms, they became aggressive on the territory of their more powerful and warlike neighbors, the Sioux, and gradually drove them westward and southward, so that fifty years ago, when Protestant Missions were first commenced among them, they were in the possession of Yellow Lake and Sandy Lake and Leech Lake and Red Lake, places that had been occupied by bands of the Dakotas.

Mr. Frederick Ayer was the first Protestant missionary teacher who visited the Ojibwas at LaPointe. In the summer of 1830, Mr. Warren, whose trading post was on Magdalen Island, came to Mackinaw with an extra boat, for the purpose of taking back with him a missionary. Mr. Ayer, the teacher of the boys' school, was then the only available person. Accordingly, with one of the scholars of the school for interpreter, he accompanied Mr. Warren to his port, surveyed the field and immediately opened a school. This he appears to have continued during the winter, and to have gone back to Mackinaw the next season with Mr. Warren.

In the meantime the American Board had commissioned Rev. Sherman Hall and his wife and Rev. William T. Boutwell, all of New England, and instructed them to proceed to establish Missions at LaPointe and elsewhere among the Ojibwas.

At this time there was residing at Mackinaw, Doctor James, Surgeon of the U. S. army, who was skilled in the language of the Ojibwas, and who had already done something in the way of translating portions of the New Testament. Mr. Boutwell elected to stop there for awhile and take lessons in the language.

On the 4th day of August, 1831, Mr. and Mrs. Hall and Mr. Ayer embarked with the company of the Fur Trade, five boats and about seventy persons, and arrived at Mr. Warren's station at LaPointe on the 30th of the same month. It is a little remarkable that such a caravan of traders should rest on the Sabbath as they did. Thus in the Providence of God a Protestant Mission was now established where one hundred and sixty-six years before the Jesuits had raised the banner of the Cross.

In the summer of 1832, Mr. Boutwell made an extensive tour, with H. R. Schoolcraft, United State Indian agent, among the Ojibwa villages scattered between Lake Superior and the sources of the Mississippi river. While on this journey, as Mr. Boutwell has since stated, they entered a lake with their canoe which they had good reason to believe was the true source of the Father of Waters. Resting upon their oars, and searching for some name to express the thought they had, Mr. Boutwell said, "Veritas Caput," from which Henry R. Schoolcraft cut out Itasca.

In the autumn of 1832, Mr. Ayer went to Sandy Lake near the Mississippi, and opened a school at the trading post of Mr. Aitkin; and Mr. Boutwell joined Mr. Hall at La Pointe. They gave themselves to learning the language, to teaching the school which was there altogether in English, and to visiting from house to house. They describe the natives as very poor, often suffering for the necessaries of life—living on fish, wild rice, sugar and wild meat. They were idle and wasteful, and consequently often in want. Poorly clad, poorly housed in their birch bark wigwams, and poorly fed, filthy and dirty in the extreme, could these savages be civilized and christianized? The full answer will have to come after many years. In the meantime these missionaries will give their best life to them. They will learn the language and prepare school books in it. They will sing hymns of praise to Christ, some of which they find already in the language, prepared by the Methodist Episcopal Missionaries in Canada; and by and by, they will preach to them in their own tongue and tell them of Jesus. Even at this time they speak of being helped by some converts to Christianity who came up from Mackinaw.

In the Report of the Board for 1833, other helpers are mentioned, as, Edmund F. Ely, Mrs. Ayer, Miss Cook, Miss Stevens, and Miss Crooks. Mr. and Mrs. Ayer with Miss Crooks opened a new station at Yellow Lake; Mr. Boutwell and Mr. Ely take up the work at Sandy Lake, and Mr. Boutwell looks over to Leech Lake and prepares to occupy that field the next year, by marrying Miss Hester Crooks. Then Mr. Ely leaves Sandy Lake and opens a station at Fond du Lac, near the head of Lake Superior. At every place they sow some seeds which will bear some fruit after many days. Mr. Ayer's effort, at Yellow Lake, is on the plan of separating those who desire to be educated and adopt civilized habits, from their heathen neighbors, and it is in a good measure successful. Such are of course persecuted and opposed by their heathen relations, and they are branded with the name of "Praying Indians." Some such there are already. During the winter of 1835-6, both at LaPointe and Yellow Lake there was much religious interest. Several conversions are mentioned at each place.

In the spring of 1836, the mission of Mr. Ayer was removed from Yellow Lake to Pokeguma. This was deemed to be, on all accounts, the most favorable place to commence a civilized community. The lake called Pokeguma, though small, was well stocked with fish, and was connected by a short channel with Snake creek and the St. Croix, and so with the Mississippi. They were, here, but two days and a half by canoe from St. Peter's (now Mendota), which became the base of supplies. In the summer of 1837, while we were stopping at the Lake Harriet station, we were rejoiced to meet Mr. Ayer and an Ojibwa native convert, at our first celebration of the Lord's supper in Dakota land. At this time, Mr. Ayer had the assistance of Mr. John L. Seymour, and the work went on bravely, both here and at the other stations. At LaPointe, Mr. Hall was supported by Mr. Joseph Town and wife. Mr. Ely of Fond du Lac was married to Miss Bissel of Mackinaw, and had for his assistant Mr. Granville T. Sproat; while Mr. and Mrs. Boutwell labored alone at Leech Lake. In the judgment of missionaries, the prospects were very encouraging,

Mr. Town appears to have remained but a little while at LaPointe, as in the Report of the Board for this year 1837, his name is omitted, and Mr. Sproat has gone to LaPointe, leaving Mr. Ely alone at Fond du Lac.

In the spring of 1838, other changes were made. At Leech Lake, as recorded, "Mr. Boutwell had little encouragement in his labors, and at times, was greatly annoyed by the savage and violent conduct of the Indians." Then Mr. and Mrs. Boutwell withdrew to Pokeguma, and Mr. and Mrs. Ayer went to Fond du Lac for a time. During this year, the gospel of John and the Acts of the Apostles were printed in the language of the Ojibwas. Luke had been printed previously. The gospel had been taking effect, especially in the little civilized (partly) community of Pokeguma. Seven couples had been married; a number had erected houses, and were living somewhat like white people, while eight or ten persons were regarded, in the judgment of charity, as christians. Quite a spiritual quickening had been experienced during the winter preceding. But, as was natural, this very progress of the gospel aroused the opposition of the heathen party, who proceeded greatly to annoy the missionaries, by killing their cattle, and threatening to drive them from the country. This was partly owing also to the fact that they had ceded to the United States in the summer of 1838, a portion of this land, and immediately, before the Treaty was ratified, white people began to take possession.

When this trouble had passed, as was supposed, and christian Indians and missionaries were hopeful again, suddenly war came upon them. The Ojibwas and Sioux were immemorial enemies. Peace was made only to be broken.

In the early spring of 1838, Hole-in-the-Day with a party had come over to the Chippewa river near Lacquiparle. They came to three teepees of Sioux, who entertained them in princely style with a dog-feast. They lay down to rest, but arose and killed their entertainers.

In retiring from this treacherous massacre, the party of Hole-in-the-Day took one women prisoner. Elder Alfred Brunson, of Prairie du Chien, was at this time establishing Methodist Missions among both the Sioux and Ojibwas. In the first days of July 1838, he passed Sauk Rapids and Little Falls, and reached the village of Hole-in-the-Day, while the agent was holding a council with the Indians about returning this Sioux captive. As Mr. Brunson represents the matter, Hole-in-the-Day himself was the last to consent to her return, because he "hated the Sioux." But finally the matter was arranged and the agent took the Sioux woman down to Fort Snelling, and she was restored to her friends. In a week or ten days after, for what reason is not apparent, Hole-in-the-Day took five braves and went down to Fort Snelling. They were quartered at Baker's stone house a mile from the Fort. Their presence becoming known to the Sioux, two young men secreted themselves and fired upon the first man who made his appearance. This happened to be an Ottawa who was living among the Ojibwas. The party of Hole-in-the-Day sallied forth and killed two Sioux. The white soldiers interfered and prevented a general war.

In June of 1839, a thousand Ojibwas came to Fort Snelling. They were under the protection of the military and so the Ojibwas and Sioux fraternised. They started home in two companies, by Rum river and the St. Croix. The night after they left, two Ojibwa young men,* to avenge the killing of their father, waylaid and killed a Dakota man on the shores of Lake Harriet. This made the war spirit boil in the hearts of the Dakotas. Two war-parties. were made up to follow the Ojibwas, and more than ninety scalps were brought home. One of the battles was fought where Stillwater now stands, which had its influence on the little settlement at Pokeguma. By these occurrences three Mission stations were eventually broken up—the station of the American Board at Lake Harriet, and the one at Pokeguma; and the Methodist Mission station at Little Crow's village.

SECTION II.

MISSION OF THE AM. BOARD WITH THE SIOUX, 1835.

The Sioux or Dakotas were the enemies of the Ojibwas. Hence it is supposed they were called, by tribes farther

---

*Said to be nephews of the man killed the year before.

—7

east, "Nadouessioux." But the Ojibwas proper called the Dakotas by the name of "Bwan," which is perpetuated in the name Assinaboine. On the other hand the Dakotas named the Ojibwas "Hahatonwan," *Dwellers at the Falls*— not the falls of St. Anthony, but of the St. Louis river, probably, or the falls of Sault Ste Marie.

Mr. Jedediah D. Stevens and wife had come, from central New York, in the summer of 1827, to the mission station at Mackinaw, where they continued two years. In the summer of 1829, Mr. Stevens was sent on an exploring tour among the Ojibwas of Wisconsin, and to the Dakotas of the Mississippi river. This journey was extended to Fort Snelling. But after his return, he and his wife labored with the Stockbridge Indians on Fox river, near Green Bay. In 1834, they were commissioned by the Am. Board to commence a Mission among the Dakotas, but they were prevented, by circumstances, from reaching Fort Snelling until the spring of 1835, and spent the winter preceding at Mackinaw.

Thomas Smith Williamson, M. D., was the son of Rev. William Williamson and Mary Smith, and was born in Union District, South Carolina, in March, 1800. He was converted during his stay at Jefferson College, Cannonsburg, Pa., where he graduated in 1820. Soon after he began reading medicine with his brother-in-law, Dr. William Wilson, of West Union, O., and after a very full course of reading, considerable practical experience, and one course of lectures at Cincinnati, O., completed his medical education at Yale, where he graduated in medicine in 1824. He settled at Ripley, O., where he soon acquired an extensive practice, and, April 10, 1827, was united in marriage with Margaret Poage, daughter of Col. James Poage.

Dr. Williamson continued in the successful practice of medicine nearly ten years, but in the spring of 1833 he placed himself under the care of the Chillicothe Presby- tery and commenced the study of theology. In August of that year he removed with his family to Walnut Hills and connected himself with Lane Seminary. In April, 1834, in the first Presbyterian Church of Red Oak. he was licensed to preach by the Chillicothe Presbytery.

Previous to his licensure he had received from the American Board an appointment to proceed on an explor- ing tour among the Indians of the upper Mississippi, with special reference to the Sacs and Foxes, but to collect what information he could in regard to the Sioux, Winne- bagoes, and other Indians. Starting on this tour about the last of April, he went as far as Fort Snelling, and returned to Ohio in August. At Rock Island he met with some of the Sacs and Foxes, and at Prairie du Chien he first saw Dakotas, among others Mr. Joseph Renville, of Lacquiparle. On the 18th of September he was ordained as a missionary by the Chillicothe Presbytery, in Union Church. Ross county, Ohio.

A few months afterward he received his appointment as a missionary of the A. B. C. F. M., to the Dakotas; and on the first day of April, 1835, Dr. Williamson, with his wife and one child, accompanied by Miss Sarah Poage, Mrs. Williamson's sister, who afterward became Mrs. Gid eon H. Pond, and Alexander G. Huggins and family, left Ripley, Ohio, and on the 16th of May they arrived at Fort Snelling.

But a year previous to this, in the spring of 1834, two brothers from Washington, Conn., Samuel W. and Gideon H. Pond, had come self-moved, or rather God-moved, to the land of the Dakotas. When they reached Fort Snelling and had made known their errand to the commanding officer of the post, Maj. Bliss, and to the resident Indian agent, Maj. Taliaferro, they received the hearty approval and co-operation of both, and the Agent at] once recommended them to commence work with the Dakotas of the Lake Calhoun village, where some steps had already been taken in the line of civilization. There, on the margin of the lake, they built their log cabin.

While stopping there for a few weeks, Dr. Williamson presided at the organization, on the 12th of June, of the First Presbyterian Church—the first Christian church organized within the present limits of Minnesota. This was within the garrison at Fort Snelling, and consisted of 22 members, chiefly the result of the labors of Major Loomis among the soldiers.

Having concluded to accompany Mr. Joseph Renville, Dr. Williamson's party embarked on the Fur Company's Mackinaw boat on the 22d of June; reached Traverse des Sioux on the 30th, where they took wagons and arrived at Lacquiparle on the 9th of July. There, on the north side of the Minnesota river, and in sight of the "Lake that speaks," they established themselves as teachers of the religion of Jesus.

Mr. Stevens immediately proceeded to erect Mission buildings, on the margin of Lake Harriet, in the vicinity of the village at Lake Calhoun, and opened a small Boarding School, which, for several years, was taught successfully by Miss Lucy C. Stevens, a niece of Rev. Mr. Stevens. Thus the Mission of the American Board among the Dakotas was fully commenced. The brothers Pond had spent the previous year in learning the language and helping the Indians. Mr. Gideon H. Pond aided Mr. Stevens in the erection of the Mission buildings, and the next year was transferred to the station at Lacquiparle, where he was married to Miss Sarah Poage and remained until the spring of 1839. Mr. Samuel W. Pond went back to Connecticut in the autumn of 1836, where he was licensed and ordained as a missionary to the Indians, and soon after his return his name was placed on the Roll of the American Board.

On the 1st day of June, 1837, the writer of this article, born in Ohio, and graduated at Jefferson College, Pa., with his wife, born in Massachusetts, and educated in the schools of Miss Lyon and Miss Grant, arrived at Fort Snelling, as missionaries of the American Board to the Dakotas. They were kindly entertained by Lieut. Ogden, in the garrison, and soon proceeded to the station at Lake Harriet, where they spent the summer, and then were transferred to Lacquiparle.

From the commencement, the work at this station was very promising. Mr. Joseph Renville, the Bois Brule trader at this place, was earnestly desirous to have his own family educated, so that as soon as possible after their arrival, Miss Poage commenced teaching a class in English. Mr. Renville himself professed to be a christian, and in less than a year, Dr. Williams had organized a native church, which, in the autumn of 1837, when I joined the mission force at Lacquiparle, counted seven Dakotas. Five years after, the number received from the beginning had been forty-nine. This was a very successful commencement.

The language of the Dakotas existed only in sounds. It was to be written. During the three years of occupancy before my arrival, the system of notation had been, in the main, determined upon; though a number of changes have since been made. The brothers Pond rightly claim the honor of teaching the first Dakota to read and write his own language. Mr. Samuel Pond thus tells the story: "In the spring of 1835, while my brother and I lived at Lake Calhoun, a young Dakota named Maza-hda-ma-ne came to our house and asked us whether we thought Dakotas could learn to read. There was then nothing printed in the Dakota language, and we had only a short time before arranged an alphabet in which it could be written; so that we could furnish him with lessons only by writing them with a pen. It was not much trouble to teach him, for he learned rapidly, both to read and write, and was soon able to write letters to us which we could understand very well, so far as we then were acquainted with the language."

Previous to this time, some efforts had been made by officers of the army and others, to write the language by the English alphabet alone, and a collection of four or five hundred words had been made. When we commenced learning the Dakota language in the summer of 1837, this collection, together with one made by Rev. J. D. Stevens, the result doubtless, in great measure, of the gathering by the Messrs. Pond, came into our hands. And, when to these were added what Dr. Williams had gathered, the vocabulary amounted to over two thousand words, which was the nucleus of the Dakota grammar and dictionary I published fourteen years after.

The mission station at Lake Harriet, which was established with the band of Dakotas then most advanced in civilization, was not destined to continue long. The fresh outbreak of the war-spirit, and the triumphant battles of the Sioux, fought with the Ojibwas in midsummer of 1839, referred to in treating of the Ojibwa mission, were fatal to the occupation of the village on Lake Calhoun. The Indians were afraid to remain there longer, and so moved over to the Minnesota river. Thereupon Mr. Stevens, receiving the appointment of farmer for Wabasha's band, living near where Winona now stands, withdrew from the service of the Board. In the summer of 1842, he was preaching to white people at Prairie [du Chien. Mr. G. H. Pond accepted the position of farmer for the Lake Calhoun band. He and his brother occupied the mission houses at Lake Harriet for a while, and then took up quarters near the Fort, where they resided until they established their station in 1842, at Oak Grove, eight miles up the Minnesota.

At Lac qui Parle among the Dakotas, the same kind of obstacles had to be met that are spoken of by the missionaries among the Ojibwas. The winter of 1838-9 Dr. Williamson spent in Ohio, getting some printing done. By the aid of Mr. Joseph Renville the gospel of Mark had been translated from the French. This was the first printing of any portion of the Bible in the Dakota language. Before his return in the summer of 1839, Eagle Help went on the war-path to avenge the killing of the three families a year previous. The mission strongly advised against the war party, and in return we had several of our cattle killed. This form of opposition was carried to such an extent, in the next few years, as to make it well nigh impossible for the missionary to remain. But in the meantime, notwithstanding the persecutions that came upon them, some Dakota men were receiving education and seeds of gospel truth, which began to germinate and bring forth some fruit.

When Dr. Williamson returned from Ohio, he brought with him Miss Fanny Huggins, who afterwards became Mrs. Jonas Pettijohn. It was thought that some manufacturing industries might profitably be introduced among the Dakota women. Accordingly several spinning wheels, both for flax and wool, were purchased by the mission. Mr. Renville had a flock of sheep, the remnant of a drove lost by a white man some years before. Mr. Huggins sowed the seed and raised the flax. He also made a loom for weaving. Thus the materials and the machinery were furnished the Indian women, to spin yarn, knit stockings, and weave cloth for short gowns, skirts and blankets. Mr. Huggins and Miss Fanny gave a good deal of time to teaching these industries, and with very considerable success. Quite a number of women made articles for their own and others use. This effort had its place in the civilizing influences, but it could not be made profitable. One that was less pretentious in the commencement has borne much larger fruit, to-wit: Teaching the Dakota women *to wash*. It had been their custom to put on a garment and wear it until it could be worn no longer. They were quite ignorant of the gospel of soap, as well as of the gospel of salvation. Mrs. Riggs had been less accustomed than some others to do the hard work of the wash-tub. Hence she was more willing to give time and patience to the education of Indian women in this line. At first it was impossible to obtain any but the lowest of the Dakota women for this service. But by and by it became popular, and has done much for their elevation.

Thus the work of education was carried on at Lac qui-Parle. In the mean time a good deal of work was done in the line of Bible translation and the preparation of books. Under date of May 10, 1842, Dr. Williamson wrote thus to the Prudential Committee: "Much of the time of Mr. Riggs and myself, for a year past, has been employed in this business, though most of the translating was done more than a year ago. Beside preparing a small Dakota hymn book and some school books, he has translated the Acts of the Apostles, the book of Revelation, and all the Epistles of Paul, also about one-third of the Psalms. He has also copied and prepared for the press the Gospel of John and a number of Psalms translated by Mr. Renville. I have carefully read over his translations and made suggestions, and he has done the same for me in respect to the book of Genesis. which I have translated." To the above was added the Gospel of Luke, translated by Mr. G. H. Pond. To oversee the printing of them in Boston and Cincinnati, the Board authorized me to make a visit east. We left one child and took two with us. On our return in the spring of 1843, we were authorized to commence a new station, which we did in June, at Traverse des Sioux.

SECTION III.

THE SWISS MISSION AMONG THE DAKOTAS, 1836 TO 1846.

About the same time that the American Board determined to send missionaries to the Dakotas, two young
men, Rev. Daniel Gavin and Rev. Samuel Denton, were
appointed by a society at Basle, in Switzerland, as missionaries to the Indians of North America. They selected
as their field of labor the land of the Dakotas. Both
were unmarried when they came to this country; but
before commencing his labors with the Dakotas, Mr.
Denton was married to Miss Paris Skinner, who had,
for several years, been engaged in the service of the
American Board at the mission school at Mackinaw. In
1839, Mr. Gavin married Miss Lucy C. Stevens, at Lake
Harriet.

They first located at Trempeleau, with the Wabasha
band of Sioux; but the next year Mr. and Mrs. Denton
removed to Red Wing, where Mr. Gavin soon afterwards
joined them. In the autumn of 1838, Mr. Gavin came up
to Lac qui Parle and spent the winter with us, giving
aid in our work of translating and other missionary labor.
From the following spring the two families were associa-
ted at Red Wing, until 1845, when Mrs. Gavin's ill-health
compelled them to leave the Dakotas. Thenceforward
Mr. Gavin labored with success among the French Cath-
olics in Canada, until his death, which occurred about
1859. Mr. Denton remained a few years after Mr. Gavin's
departure, when he too was obliged to leave on account
of ill-health, and died soon after in Missouri.

While the Dentons were still at Red Wing's village,
in the summer of 1846, the present writer made a canoe

voyage, with his wife, down the Mississippi, and stopped for ten days with them, at the Wood-Water-Hill village. Here I remember visiting a young man who was sick, and who now is the stalwart and honored pastor of our Santee Agency Mission church—Rev. Artemas Ehnamane. So that, if the question "cui bono," is asked in regard to the ten years of the Swiss mission, I reply: It was a time of seed sowing. Quite a number of children and young folks learned to read more or less in both English and Dakotah; and many older ones heard prayer and instruction from the word of God, from these earnest workers. The harvest came a score of years afterwards in the prison and in the camp.*

SECTION IV.

MISSIONS OF THE METHODIST EPISCOPAL CHURCH, AMONG THE SIOUX AND OJIBWAS, 1837.

Early in the present century the Methodists embarked in missions among the Indians. In 1819, John Steward, a free colored man, commenced a successful religious and educational work among the Wyandots, on the upper Sandusky. The influence of this effort extended over into Canada, to others of the Hurons. John Sunday and John and Peter Jones, of the Ojibwa tribe, were converted and became active helpers. This was in 1823. In 1830, and onward, we find John Sunday and George Copway and others, going on missionary tours on Lake Superior. In 1833, they established a successful and permanent mission at L'Anse, on Kewenaw bay, in Michigan. Here was commenced a civilized and Christian community—

*The statements in regard to the mission are, many of them, taken from an article furnished by Rev. S. W. Pond, and published in the Iapi Oaye of April, 1874.

the Indians laying by their annuity money, after 1842,. to enter their lands as white men. Of these and other missions, Rev. John Clark, whose headquarters were at. Sault Ste. Marie, was the Superintendent.

Rev. Alfred Brunson, of the Pittsburg Conference, had become interested in the Indians of the Northwest, by reading Lieut. Allen's account of his voyage with School-craft, when on search of the head of the Mississippi. He communicated this interest to the conference at its. meeting in July, 1835, and receiving an appointment to that work, he immediately set out on horse back and traveled through the states of Ohio, Indiana and Illinois, and up to Fort Crawford, at Prairie du Chien. In the winter he rode back to his home in the Meadville district, and found his family ready with a boat to remove in the early spring. It was the middle of July when they reached Prairie du Chien, too late to commence operations in the Indian country. But in the meantime Mr. Brunson, considering that an interpreter was needed in commencing mission work among the Sioux, and learning that James Thompson, a slave, who had a Sioux woman for a wife, was with his master, an officer, at Fort Snelling, and could be purchased for $1,200, he wrote on to his friends in the east. This was the time when the anti-slavery feeling ran highest in Ohio, and multitudes of people were only too glad to contribute to the fund that was started in Cincinnati, for the purpose of obtaining for James Thompson his liberty, that he might serve in the Methodist church in giving the gospel to the Sioux nation. No doubt this transaction had a. good result in keeping the anti-slavery fires burning brightly, but as a missionary investment it was an act of very doubtful utility. So it appeared to us of the Presbyterian mission. Thompson was a very indifferent interpreter and not a reliable man, and so was dismissed from the mission before its disbandment.

During the winter of 1836-7, Elder Brunson made his arrangements, and on the 19th of May, embarked on a steamboat for Fort Snelling. After consulting with the agent and officers of the garrison, the village of Kaposia, six or eight miles below the Fort, on the west side of the Mississippi, was the place selected for their first station. This was long known as "Little Crow's village." At this time the name of the chief was Wamde-tanka, *Big Eagle*. His father's name was Chatan-wakoowa-mani — " *Who-walks-pursuing-a-hawk*,"—from which "Little Crow" seems to have been taken. The dynasty became extinct in Ta-oyati-doota—the Little Crow of the outbreak of 1862.

Superintendent Brunson had with him David King, as teacher, with his family, and a farmer and his family, with Jim, the interpreter, and a hired man. Immediately they commenced to erect mission buildings of logs. Elder Brunson returned to Prairie du Chien for supplies, and in his second trip up he took with him George Copway, John Johnson and Peter Marksman, three young Ojibwas, who had been converted in Upper Canada, under the labors of Peter Jones and William Case. More recently they had been employed by Rev. John Clark in the Indian missions of Ottawa and Lac Court Orilles, in Wisconsin. They were t) go down to the Methodist mission school at Jacksonville, Illinois, but in the meantime they could put in some months work on the upper Mississippi. The Sioux could hardly believe that they were Ojibwas, for they worked, they said, like Frenchmen. In September of that year a treaty was made with the Ojibwas by Governor Dodge, at Fort Snelling. Mr. Brunson and his three young Ojibwa converts were present, and made a good impression.

At the conference which met at Jacksonville, in October, 1837, supplies were voted to carry on the new missions, and Rev. T. W. Pope and Rev. James G. Whitford, with Hiram Delap, were added to his force of workers. These new men went immediately up to the station at Kaposia, while Elder Brunson purchased supplies. The row boat which took up these was frozen up in the middle of November, and they had to be transported on the ice, from the lower end of Lake Pepin.

Early in May, 1838, Superintendent Brunson took a steamboat and went to visit the Sioux mission. He found that the mission had wintered comfortably — the school under Mr. King, had been somewhat successful — and the spring work, for the Indians, was prosecuted with such vigor that more than 100 acres of land was ploughed for them, to the great delight of the Indians. In their school, contrary to the practice of the other missions among the Sioux, they determined to teach only English.

At this time the war spirit ran high at Little Crow's village, in consequence of the three families killed in April, near Lac qui Parle, by Hole-in-the-Day. But nevertheless. Mr. Brunson, with three white men and his interpreter, started in the last days of June, up the Mississippi, to visit the Ojibwas and arrange for the establishment of a mission among the Ojibwas. They reached Crow Wing, the village of Hole-in-the-Day, while the question of returning the

Sioux captive woman was being discussed. Mr. Brunson represents Hole-in-the-Day, the dirtiest and most savage-looking of them all, as not being willing for her delivery for some time; and finally yielding under pressure. In the then excited state of affairs the missionary company did no more at this time than examine some localities where a. mission could be established.

In the month of August, Elder Brunson took "Whitford and Randolph" with "Bungo," as Ojibwa interpreter, and started up the St. Croix to visit Lac Court Orilles. But when they had almost reached the place, some dogs, one night. ate up the bacon, and they were obliged to return. This seemed to be providential; for in the meantime, Hole-in-the-Day had come down to Fort Snelling with a, few men. One of these had been shot by the Sioux, and they in turn killed two of their enemies. Whereupon, to keep the party of Hole-in-the-Day from being entirely cut. off, the commandant of the garrison took them within its walls. This greatly enraged the Sioux, who were now planning to attack the Fort also. In this storm of excitement the occupants of the mission got some of their effects. into a large bark canoe, and would have fled down the Mississippi; but Little Crow commanded them back to their house—placed his son, the third Little Crow, as guard over them, and assured them of safe protection. The next. day, unexpectedly to them all, Elder Brunson returned. They talked and prayed over the situation, and concluded that it was safe for them to lie down and sleep under the protection of the Great Father above. But the Elder himself went out by night to see the *Scalp Dance.*

When Superintendent Brunson returned to Prairie du.

Chien that fall, Hiram Delap and family, Witt Randolph returned with him. He went down to Alton, Illinois, and attended conference, and then purchased supplies for the mission and went up on the steamer "Gypsy," where as passengers he met Dr. Emerson and wife, with the afterwards famous "Dred Scott," as their slave. From this trip Elder Brunson returned home sick and did not wholly recover for several years.

In the mean time the good Methodist people, not considering that a mission to savage Indians is not a harvest field in which they could reap immediately, nor even "a prairie farm," from which a crop might be expected in two or three years, but real scrub-and-grab land, which required an immense amount of hard work before the harvest came, became dissatisfied, and complained that there were no results and a great expenditure. This was unreasonable, but Methodism then had not learned to work and wait for fruit in such unpromising fields.

In the summer of 1839, Rev. Mr. Pope's health having failed, he left the mission as Elder Brunson resigned his superintendency, and Rev. B. T. Kavenaugh was appointed in his place.

Among the "same fruit" in the spiritual harvest of the first years of this mission work, Mr. Bennron mentions the conversion of one Jacob Fallstrum and his family. As a Swedish boy Fallstrum had come over to Lord Selkirk's settlement, married a half Ojibwa woman and worked his way down to the neighborhood of Fort Snelling. As he talked the Ojibwa language they made him a preacher to his wife's people.

Immediately after his appointment, Elder Kavenaugh proceeded to his missionary field, taking with him Rev. Samuel Spates, Rev. Mr. Huddleston, Rev. John Johnson and Rev. Peter Marksman—the two latter native Ojibwas. With them he proceeded up the Mississippi and established a Mission at Elk River on the east bank of the Mississippi. There on the 30th of December, 1839, Mr. Huddleston died of dysentery and was buried on the top of a hill overlooking the river. It is recorded, that Hole-in-the-Day cast a heap of stones on his grave, "to mark the place where the good man lies, who came to bless us."

In the fall of 1840 a new Mission was established at Sandy Lake under the charge of Mr. Spates. Owing to the incursions of Sioux war parties, Hole-in-the-Day's village was deserted, and the Mission removed in February of 1840 to Rabbit river. But this appears to have been very soon abandoned and stations formed farther in the interior—at White Fish Lake and Fond du Lac of Lake Superior. In Judge Gale's "Upper Mississippi" this statement is made in regard to this mission: "In July, 1841, the Missions were consolidated into that at Sandy Lake, in charge of Rev. H. J. Bruce and Rev. Samuel Spates, with a school of thirty scholars; that at White Fish Lake, in charge of Rev. John Johnson; and that at Fond du Lac, in charge of Rev. George Copway, with his wife and her sister and James Simpson, as teachers.*

---

* I am sorry that I have not been able to obtain reliable materials for tracing this Ojibwa branch of the Methodist mission to its close.

—8

The mission among the Sioux at Kaposia was much annoyed by the war parties in the spring of 1841 and the school was closed by order of Little Crow. Mr. Holton and his family had, before this time, retired from the Mission and made a home on the other side of the Mississippi in the edge of Red Rock prairie. Others perhaps settled on the same prairie. The Indians became insolent and exacting. Perhaps they had been spoiled from the beginning by having too much done for them by the missionaries. It was reported to us that Indian men would come in the night to the mission and demand food, which the missionaries felt obliged to give. Accordingly Elder Kavenaugh put up buildings on Red Rock prairie where a school was maintained for several years for Indian half-breed and white children. This was of course a preaching station, and became the starting point for Methodism in Minnesota. As such, I leave its further history to be traced under another head.

More than any other member of our Dakota Mission, Rev. S. W. Pond had an opportunity to form the acquaintance of these Methodist missionaries. He met several of them frequently and sometimes had the pleasure of entertaining them at his house. He speaks of Rev. David King as a good man whom he knew best, as he came up with the first in 1837 and remained after the others had gone.

It is pleasant to believe that the Lord Jesus, who has said, "Go, preach the gospel," knows even the beginnings of good, and will suffer no well-meant effort to fail, but will gather all up at the revelation of that day. To us it seems as if they did not hold on until the harvest came, and the reaping has fallen mainly into other hands.

SECTION V.

MISSION OF THE AMERICAN BOARD WITH THE OJIBWAS CONTINUED: 1840—1854.

As we commence this second decade of the Mission among the Ojibwas, we find but two stations occupied. At La Pointe, are still Mr. Hall and Mr. Sproat, with their wives; and at Pokeguma, are Mr. Boutwell, Mr. Ayer and Mr. Ely, with their wives and Miss Sabrina Stevens. Mr. and Mrs. Seymour have retired from the service of the Board, and the station at Fond du Lac has been abandoned in consequence of the removal of the Indians. The Report of the Board gives this record: "The number of Indians to whom the Mission have had access, both at LaPointe and Pokeguma has been larger than heretofore, and at the latter place there is manifested an increasing desire to lead a settled life; and were it not for their hostilities with the Sioux, the prospect for improvement in their character and habits, under the influence of Christian instruction, would be highly encouraging."

At Pokeguma they had erected a pleasant log building, which gave them joy as a convenient place for school and church, in both of which their progress during the next winter was very satisfactory. But the shadow of war hung over them. In the summer of 1841, Mr. Ayer wrote to the committee in Boston: "War has desolated Pokeguma. On the 24th of May more than one hundred Sioux fell upon our quiet settlement, and in two short hours made it the

scene of war and death." It appears that three large war-
parties were made up, all to attack the village of Pokeguma. The first was headed by Little Crow, father of the
Little Crow of 1862 notoriety. At the Falls of the St. Croix
two Ojibwa young men stumbled upon them and killed two
sons of Little Crow. One of them was killed in return,
and the other carried the news to their home at Poke
guma. This party deeply chagrined at their loss returned
to Kaposia. The second party turned back from the mouth
of Snake river, and the attack was made on the village by
the third party. Two girls belonging to the Mission school,
who had gone to the farther shore of the lake in a canoe,
were killed; but the battle was mainly near the Mission
with the praying Indians, the wilder part of the band having their homes on the island. So far as taking scalps
was concerned this battle was not a success for the Sioux,
as they left more than they took. But nevertheless, the
result was, that the Indians abandoned the lake, and the
Mission there was brought to a close. As Mr. Ayer wrote,
the Sioux were resolved to blot out the name of Pokeguma.

In the meantime reinforcements for the Ojibwa Mission
were sent forward. In the summer of 1841, Rev. Leonard
H. Wheeler and Mr. Woodbridge L. James, with their wives,
and Miss Abigail Spooner, joined the station at LaPointe.
Some of the Indians fleeing from the Sioux attacks on
Pokeguma appear to have gone back to Magdalen Island.
So that, in the winter following, the schools, both for boys
and girls, were filled up and very prosperous. Mr. and
Mrs. Wheeler and Mr. Sproat taught night schools, and
thus a larger enthusiasm was created in the work of edu-

cation. On the Sabbath, they held two public religious services in Ojibwa and one in English, besides a Sabbath school. Mr. Hall wrote at this time: "Notwithstanding the troubles between the Sioux and Ojibwas, I think there never has been more encouragement to labor for the conversion of the Ojibwas, than there is at present."

Mr. James' health failed soon after their arrival at La Pointe, and they were obliged to return home. In the spring of 1842, Mr. Ely removed to Fond du Lac, whither some of the Christian Indians had fled from the Sioux war on Pokeguma. At this latter place Mr. Boutwell and Mr. Ayer still remained, and visited the Indians from time to time in their hiding places. In their winter encampments both Mr. Boutwell and Mr. Wheeler visited them and at different times administered the Lord's supper. *On one of these occasions, two new members were added to the litle band of believers. When the spring of 1843 came, the fear of their enemies had so far passed away that many of the old settlers at Pokeguma returned, pagans as well as Christians, and again cultivated their fields and occupied their houses. Of that summer Mr. Boutwell wrote: "Our place of worship has often been well filled with attentive listeners on the Sabbath; pagans have frequently attended whom I have never seen in the house of God." By the Indians living on Mille Lac, Mr. Boutwell was invited to occupy that place. but the Pokeguma band would not consent to his leaving.

In the meantime Mr. Ayer had made a winter journey through the north country, to Leech Lake west of the

---

*Mr. Wheeler's visit was in the spring of 1842, when the Indians were encamped on the lake shore near where Duluth now stands.

Mississippi, and on to Red Lake, which communicates with the Red River of the North. At Leech Lake the principal chief endeavored to persuade him to remain there, and not go beyond, saying that although there were some bad men there, the most of them were not so, and would treat missionaries well. In this he counted beyond his power, for three years after the missionaries of the A. M. A. were obliged to leave, and at a still later day the Episcopal Mission was broken up by them. Mr. Ayer pushed on to Red Lake, which he regarded as a very favorable field, and in the spring and summer of 1843, he and Mr. Ely proceeded to occupy it. In this spring of 1843, the Ojibwa missionaries, Mr. Hall, Mr. Boutwell, Mr. Ayer and Mr. Ely, all joined in a letter to the Prudential committee, asking for reinforcements, and saying that the Ojibwa country appeared to them open, as it had not done before, to the teachers of religion and letters. Partly, we may suppose, as a result of this letter, the American Missionary Association entered the Ojibwa field in this year 1843, and established several stations, as detailed in another section of this paper.

In June 1844, Mr. Wheeler communicated the particulars of a very interesting revival work, which took place at LaPointe the winter preceding. It commenced in the native church, where there was mutual confession of sin, accompanied with tears of repentance. "During the winter some twelve or fourteen professed submission to Christ" for the first time. This was cheering to the hearts of the missionaries, so that they could say: "In view of all which the Lord has done for us during the past winter, we feel greatly encouraged to go forward in our work."

In the Report of the Board for 1844, it appears that Mr. Ely is back at Pokeguma, and Mr. and Mrs. Ayer remained at Red Lake, which station was held, for a number of years, conjointly by the American Board and the A. M. A.'s Mission. The whole of the New Testament was now printed in the Ojibwa language and also a hymn book. These were grand helps in the work of evangelization; and we should not be surprised to find the preaching of the gospel taking effect, during the next two years, at the far-off station of Red Lake.   This seems to have been chiefly, though not entirely, in a family of half-bloods; an old woman of eighty, with her daughter and husband, and several of their children were among the dozen persons who were received into the church in March 1846.   For the two years previous, some of these Indians had been making rapid strides in civilization, making small plantings and building houses.   They were away from the influences of fire-water, and at this time had no resident trader among them.

The soil about La Pointe on Magdalen Island, was found to be poorly adapted to tillage. Hence in the spring of 1845, many of the Indians removed to Bad River, on the main land, about 20 miles to the southeast, where they had previously cultivated small fields, and where an agricultural settlement could be established. Mr. and Mrs. Wheeler went with them to this new settlement and commenced a mission station, which has since been called "Odonah," that is being interpreted "village."   During the next two years comfortable and substantial dwelling houses and school house and other convenient buildings were erected at this new station. The Indians also made "some progress in outward improvement" and were "much more industrious than formerly." The gospel, although it has not yet proved the power of God unto salvation to many of them, has evidently done much to soften the savage ferocity of their character." Thus wrote Mr. Wheeler in the last days of 1847.

In the meantime other important changes in the mission had taken place. The reoccupation of Pokeguma by the Indians in the summer of 1843, noticed by Mr. Boutwell, and the attendant encouraging prospects for missionary labor among them there, were not destined to be of long continuance. The country around there was now ceded, and white people began to come in and occupy it. The Indians retired before them, so that in 1845, Pokeguma as a missionary station was abandoned, Mr. Ely going to La Pointe to take Mr. Sproat's place in the school, and Mr. Boutwell being released from his connection with the Board, remained to preach the gospel to the incoming settlement of white people. After a service of fifty years, for the elevation and salvation of Indians and white people, Mr. Boutwell is still living near Stillwater.

The influx of white settlers brought evil more than good to the Ojibwas. The men who came to work the mines were neither religious nor very moral, as a class, and their influence upon the Indians was, in the first instance, debasing. At every point plenty of fire-water came into the country, and thus the red men were tempted too strongly on their weakest side. In the beginning of the year 1847, Mr. Hall wrote a letter to the Prudential committee, deploring this changed state of things, in which he expressed the belief that "nothing will prevent their

utter destruction but a thorough conversion to God."
And theirs were not the environments in which the missionaries could strongly hope for the influence of the
Holy Spirit. But dark as the prospects were, they did
not give up hope. Not in themselves, not in their schools,
not in their books, not in the gathered settlements for
civilization, Mr. Hall says, but in God, was their hope.
At Red Lake too there were dark clouds. The war spirit
was rampant, and the missionaries lamented the desertion
of several of their native church members. Even at this
remote station, from Pembina and the Red River settlement as well as from the east, the means of intoxication
flowed in upon them, and they were but too ready to
welcome the "minnewakan." Still there were hopeful
signs. The old Indians said, "Our children will all
pray." But "we cannot pray now; we must go to war
next summer; and we cannot fight and pray too." So
reasoned the Ojibwas.

In the year 1849, Rev. Frederick Ayer of Red Lake, was
released from his connection with the Board, and the station
turned over to the American Missionary Association, whose
missionaries had been there for several years. The same
year Mr. Ely also was released from his connection with
the American Board, and his place as teacher at La Pointe
was supplied by Mr. Charles Pulsifer, who with his wife
had recently joined that Mission.* For two or three years
from this time onward, the Ojibwas on the south side of
Lake Superior were kept in a state of great excitement
by orders of the government for their removal to the

---

*In the summer of 1849 Mr. Hall and Mr. Wheeler made a tour through the north
country as far as Red Lake.

Mississippi river country.   In the autumn of 1850 they
were required to go to Sandy Lake to receive their annuities.   Some went and some did not; and those who went
fared the worst, as the provisions were scanty and poor,
many sickened and died, and only some goods were distributed.   At this time Mr. Hall made a visit to that part
of the country, that he might be prepared for action in
the future.   The winter following, Mr. Wheeler, being on
a visit to New England, went with one of the secretaries
of the Board, Rev. S. B. Treat, to Washington, to repre-
sent to the Commissioner of Indian Affairs the desirable-
ness and propriety of permitting those Indians to remain
on the shores of Lake Superior.   On his return to Bad
River in the spring, he could not give the Indians any
assurance that the government would comply with their
request to remain; but he could tell them that the only
possible conditions on which they could stay were, that
they should adopt the dress and the habits of white people.*

This information and advice had a good effect.   The Indians were put on their character.   They planted more.
They did not make dances.   They sent their children to
school, and they themselves came to church.   And they
greatly abstained from intoxicating drinks.   The church at
La Pointe now numbered 22, some of whom were white
persons.   On the whole the missionaries had a good many
things to encourage them.

The government persisted in the plan of removing the
La Pointe Indians to the Mississippi.   In 1852, Mr. Hall was
requested to take charge of a boarding school, to be commenced on the left bank of the Crow Wing River, about

* See Mr. Wheeler's letter in the Herald of Oct., 1851.

ten miles from its junction with the Mississippi, under the auspices of the U. S. government. In September he visited the place, and being pleased with the prospects, he removed his family thither in the following spring; and was accompanied by Mr. Pulsifer and Henry Blatchford, a native catechist. The station at La Pointe having been occupied now more than twenty years, was abandoned. Mr. Wheeler was left in charge of the whole mission work on the lake shore. The effort to remove these Indians was so distasteful to them that the government finally abandoned the plan. This left Mr. Hall and his companions on the Crow Wing, with so few Ojibwas about them, and with so much firewater and so many Sioux war parties, that the attempt of the government to establish there a boarding school was abandoned.

In the year 1854, Rev. Sherman Hall, having been almost a quarter of a century in the service of the American Board among the Ojibwas, retired from that service, and thenceforth gave himself to home mission work. Mr. Hall died Aug. 31, 1879, at Sauk Rapids, Minn.

The effort of the government to remove the Indians from Lake Superior having been given up, the annual payment was made there in the autumn of 1853. The Indians were well pleased with the change of plan, and became from that time more desirous to come under the conditions of civilization and Christianity. The next year Mr. Wheeler represents as "one of progress;" "a number of Indians," he says, "including three chiefs, have identified themselves with the Christian party, and call themselves 'Praying Indians.'"

SECTION VI.

MISSIONS OF THE AMERICAN BOARD WITH THE SIOUX— CONTINUED—1843.

In the month of June, 1843, the new station at Traverse des Sioux was commenced. There accompanied us, from Ohio, Mr. Robert Hopkins and his young wife, Agnes, Miss Jane S. Williamson, sister of Dr. Williamson, and Miss Julia Kephart. Also, there came from Massachusetts, Thomas L. Longley, a brother of Mrs. Riggs, in the strength of his young manhood. Aunt Jane Williamson, as we all learned to call her, stopped with her brother at Fort Snelling. The Doctor had spent the year previous at that point in the place of Mr. S. W. Pond, who was at Lac qui Parle. And he had arranged with the surgeon of the post to spend a few months in the garrison during the summer. Consequently Mr. and Mrs. Hopkins pro ceeded, for the year, to Lac qui Parle, as Mr. Pond had already come down. Mrs. Riggs went up with the party to bring down our little girl. They had the bad fortune to fall in with an Ojibwa war party at Chippewa river, who had just kill and scalped two Sioux on their way out to meet friends.

The young man, Thomas Longley, remained with me at the Traverse, to erect a log cabin. A part of the Indians at that place were favorable to our commencing a station there, and a part were opposed to it. But we trusted they would come around all right. Before our cabin was ready to be occupied, and only a few days after Mrs. Riggs had returned from Lac qui Parle, Thomas Longley, while bathing in the Minnesota river, was drowned. The Indians of the opposition said that "Oonktayhe", their Neptune, was angry with us missionaries, and this was made a justification for their killing the yoke of oxen we had. A third ox, which I purchased to haul wood with the next winter, went the same way, the following summer. Besides, this was the commencement of the flooding of the Minnesota country with fire-water, by white men. The Indians at the Traverse were drunk most of the time, and our house was often visited by them in a state of intoxication. Doubtless we should have been justified by most persons if we had abandoned the station. But we held on—made a little progress in the education of children—built a chapel, and had some listeners to the preaching of the gospel.

At Lac qui Parle the opposition took the same form as at the Traverse—that of killing Mission cattle. For a while it seemed as if the Lac qui Parle station would have to be given up for lack of means of transportation. In the month of March, 1846, Mr. Joseph Renville died. He had been such a good friend of the Mission for about eleven years, could it be carried on now without him, and against so much opposition? Dr. Williamson may have felt doubtful. At any rate, when he received an invitation, that summer from Little Crow's band, to come down and establish a school and Mission at Kaposia, where the Methodist Mission had been a few years before, he regarded it as a call from God, and went. This made it necessary for me to return to Lac qui Parle, although, having suffered so much at the Traverse, it was hard to feel quite satisfied to leave a place so consecrated. But the hand of God was in it. Thencefoward there was less of opposition, and great success attended our Mission work. Dr. Williamson built at Kaposia. The brothers Pond had become located at Oak Grove—Samuel W. soon after this time branched off to the village of Shakopee. Mr. Hopkins and Mr. A. G. Huggins occupied at the Traverse; and Mr. Jonas Pettijohn, who had married Miss Fanny Huggins, was with us at Lac qui Parle.

In these years St. Paul was in its infancy and noted only for its grog shops. Dr. Williamson, living near by, preached the first sermon (Protestant) in the place, and was instrumental in having Miss Harriet E. Bishop, one of Gov. Slade's girls, come out there as the first school teacher.

At all our stations the work of education and evangelization appeared more hopeful. Mr. Robert Hopkins and Mr. G. H. Pond were licensed and ordained by the Dakota Presbytery, organized in the fall of 1844. In the summer of 1848 the board sent out several additional workers — Rev. M. N. Adams, Rev. John F. Aiton, Rev. Joseph W. Hancock and Rev. Joshua Potter. The latter came up from the Cherokee country and did not remain long, as the Sioux field did not look inviting. Mr. Hancock and Mr. Aiton occupied Red Wing, which had been vacated by the Swiss missionaries. Mr. and Mrs. Adams spent several years at Lac qui Parle, starting a small family boarding school. Thus the work made some progress, but hardly in proportion to our enlarged force of workers.

Then came the summer of 1851, with its treaties of Traverse des Sioux and Minnesota, by which the white people got possession of the State of Minnesota, and the

Indians were removed to the Reserve on the upper part of the Minnesota river. This arrangement was followed by many changes in our Dakota Mission. Even before the treaties were ratified, white people began to come into the newly ceded territory. The Indians were shortly removed from the Mississippi and lower Minnesota. In the summer of 1852, Dr. Williamson selected a location and erected a mission house above the Yellow Medicine, which he called "Pazhehootaze." Late in the autumn he removed his family to the new station, where they had to live much by faith during the severe winter that followed.

It should have been noticed that while the Treaty of Traverse des Sioux was in its preparatory state, by a mysterious providence, Rev. Robert Hopkins was suddenly called away to the other world. On the morning of the 4th of July, 1851, he went out to bathe in the overflow of the river, and was drowned. Mr. Hopkins was a conscientious Christian man and a faithful worker in the missionary field.

When the Indians were removed from Red Wing, Oak Grove, Shakopee and Traverse des Sioux, the missionaries elected to remain and cast in their lot with the new and fast growing white communities. Thus J. W. Hancock organized, and for many years ministered to, the First Presbyterian church of Red Wing. G. H. Pond organized the Oak Grove church and was its successful pastor for twenty years. In like manner, S. W. Pond was the organizer and for many years the pastor of the Presbyterian church of Shakopee. In 1852, M. N. Adams received an invitation to come and build up the Presbyterian church at Traverse des Sioux. Thus our Indian

Missions gave of their jewels to the white people and the work of Foreign Missions *dovetailed* in with the Home Mission upbuilding.   These gifts reduced the Mission of the American Board to its lowest terms.   Could it be conducted to a successful issue with such diminished forces?   Henceforth the lesson to be learned was, "Not by might nor by power, but by my Spirit, saith the Lord."

SECTION VII.

MISSION OF THE A. M. A. WITH THE OJIBWAS, 1843 TO 1859.

The American Missionary Association, which had been formed in the interest of the colored people, by some of the best Christian men and women of the country, very soon after its organization, turned its attention to the Indians.   Their Mission among the Ojibwas of Min-nesota was commenced in the fall of 1843, by sending out from Oberlin, Ohio, Rev. Alonzo Barnard and wife; Dr. William Lewis and wife; P. O. Johnson and wife; and D. B. Spencer and S. G. Wright, who were unmarried.   At the same time Rev. J. P. Bardwell went, as blacksmith, to Sandy Lake, in the service of the government.

Mr. Barnard and wife with Mr. Spencer and S. G. Wright were located at Red Lake, to labor in connection with Rev. Frederick Ayer of the American Board. And Dr. Lewis and Mr. Johnson commenced a station at Leech Lake, where Mr. Boutwell and wife had been some years before.   But these Indians at Leech Lake were bad Indians, the Pillagers, and treated these mis-sionaries no better, (if indeed so well) than they had Mr. Boutwell.   They killed the Mission cattle, and were persistent beggars, ugly and threatening in their demands. In the fall of 1845, this station was abandoned, when P. O. Johnson and wife retired from the work, and Dr. and Mrs. Lewis were transferred to the station at Red Lake. In the previous year (1844) this Mission force at Red Lake had been further increased by Mr. O. A. Coe and wife from the States; Mr. Coe went out as farmer. But in the summer of 1847, Rev. Mr. Barnard and Mr. Spencer formed a new Station at Red Cedar or Cass Lake, which was joined the same year by Mr. A. B. Adams and wife, new missionaries. This appears to have been commenced under very favorable circumstances, as we have it on the record, that a church was formed soon after, and six Indian houses were built in the year (1848) following, when J. S. Fisher and wife and Francis Spees and wife were added to the missionary force at Cass Lake.

In the neighborhood of the Red Cedar or Cass Lake, was Lake Winnebagooshish or Winnipeg, which appears by the records to be counted as a station of the A. M. A. as early as 1849. This was dropped three years afterwards, and again taken up in the spring of 1856, the missionary laborers going from Cass Lake. In the meantime two new men joined the force at Red Lake, viz: Mr. R. M. Lafferty and Mr. E. Carver. So that, although in this year of 1851, Dr. Lewis and wife retired from the service of the Association, the next year, the Missionary workers in the employ of the Society had reached the highest number—21. When 1853 came around, Winnebagooshish was dropped, and new stations were commenced at St. Joseph and Belle Prairie and the workers were counted at nineteen.

—9

The number of men and women in this work had now begun to decrease. No additional ones came. And A. B. Adams and wife retired in the summer of 1852, and settled at Belle Prairie. And in 1854, Rev. M. Barnard and family left the work, after being in the service *eleven* years. Mr. Coe also left the same year, and settled at Belle Prairie. But notwithstanding the diminished force of laborers, a Boarding School was commenced at Red Lake.

In 1856 the Association reports four stations and seventeen missionary workers. This year mission work was renewed at Winnipeg or Winnebagooshish, and a large force sent from Red Lake and Cass Lake—Mr. Bardwell, Mr. Lafferty, Mr. Fisher, Mr. Spencer, Mr. Carver, Mr. Spees and Mr. Wright—and all had their families with them except Mr. Spees. Mr. Bardwell and Mr. Spees remained but a short time, but still there was a large force left. And this, for missionary work, under the circumstances, was a disadvantage. The Commissioner of Indian Affairs, Mr. Manypenny, with the best intentions in the world, placed in the hands of the A. M. A. and its missionaries the expenditure of not only the *educational* but the *civilization* funds of that section, thus bitterly antagonizing the missionaries with the Indian agent and the traders. The agent cursed the missionaries and told the Indians if they killed them no one would care. For missionaries to obtain the handling of government money is always a grave mistake. Added to this antagonism of the forces which should have helped each other in the work of civilization, was the fact that "fire water" was brought in by the barrel, and the Indians were drunk the greater part of the time. It is put upon the record that about this time the work of the Society at Red Lake was "suspended on account of unreasonable demands of the Indians upon the missionaries for secular labors and assistance." This is from the Society's records. It does not appear that they resumed work there for some years, although "Mr. Wright wrote of the steadfastness of the little church there."

In 1858 this record is made: "Rev. J. P. Bardwell visited the Mission and reported the Indians at Cass Lake and Winnipeg as making improvements in agriculture." But, as Mr. Wright reports: "In the spring of 1859 the Missions at all the different points, were discontinued." And the secretary of the Association writes: "It was decided to relinquish the Mission. Among the reasons were the following: 1. The anticipations of the missionaries were very far from being met. 2. The parents have so little regard for the education of their children. 3. Intemperance and the facilities for obtaining the means of intoxication increased. 4. The licentious habits of white men, and the influence of the traders."

Thus closed the work of the A. M. A. for the Ojibwas. They had occupied the field for sixteen years with a good force of workers. One counts over *one hundred and sixty years* of missionary labor performed and at an expenditure of probably not less than $50,000. And with what results? Mr. S. G. Wright, who, after his connection with the Society closed, was for many years a teacher under the government; makes this answer: 1. "A great amount of prejudice has been removed from the

minds of the Indians. When we first met the Indians
at Red Lake we found them full of prejudice against
the whites. The old chief told us he believed all white
men would lie—that they were all dishonest and were
not the friends of the Indians. I am sure the chiefs
and all the people came to regard missionaries, at least.
in a very different light. 2. Another result was, under
the influence of the Mission, the majority of the men
were induced to adopt habits of industry. In 1843, only
four men had been known to assist the women in cul-
tivating the ground. Now there are very few Indians
in the country who do not work with the ax and the
hoe. 3. Another result of these years of labor is — a
great amount of religious instruction has been given.
All through the land of the Ojibwas the gospel has
been preached — in the wigwam, by the wayside and in
the church. 4. Churches were organized at different
points, and, although we could not speak of any great
gathering, there were conversions all along, and we have
witnesses the growth of some remarkable Christian char-
acters. Many of them have passed away to join the
company of all languages and nations who are around
the throne."

Leech Lake appears to have been a hard place. First
Mr. Boutwell and wife spent several years there after
1834. Thus the mission of the A. M. A. was established
there in 1843, for two years only. Next Rev. Mr. Breck
established an Episcopal mission in 1856, but left in two
years, on account of bad treatment from the Indians.
Again at two different times, and for several years each
time, between 1860 and 1871, Mr. Wright was there as

government teacher. But in all this time no one was known to become a christian. But in 1875, Mr. Wright was again employed there as a teacher under government. This time he continued for three years and a half. And now commenced the gathering of the harvest. "From the beginning of our work," Mr. Wright says, "we had good and very attentive congregations. Some very remarkable conversions took place the first year. And from that on, there was no time when there was not considerable religious interest. Nearly forty were hopefully converted." This is a good record. "Though the blessing tarry, wait for it," is the divine command.

SECTION VIII.

MISSIONS OF THE PROTESTANT EPISCOPAL CHURCH AMONG THE OJIBWAS AND SIOUX—1852 TO 1880.

REV. JOHN JOHNSON, called by his people "*Enmegahbowh*—the one who stands before his people," was an Ottawa by birth, and had been adopted by the Ojibwas. He was converted under Methodist preaching in Canada, educated at the Methodist Mission school at Jacksonville, Illinois, and became a preacher of the gospel. In the autumn of 1839 he accompanied Elder T. B. Kavenaugh up the Mississippi river, and was thenceforward a missionary of the Methodist Episcopal church among the Ojibwas, until they withdrew from the field.

In the summer of 1852, at the solicitation of Enmegabowh, Rev. James Lloyd Breck, a minister of the Episcopal church, left St. Paul and traveled on foot up the Mississippi to the mouth of Crow Wing, and thence to the shore of Gull Lake. He had as his companion in the

journey, a young divinity student from their Seminary
at *Nashotah*, Wisconsin.   Arriving at Gull Lake, he held
a council with the chief men, a majority of whom favored
his proposition to establish a Mission and school among
them.

Under the tall pine trees of Gull Lake, he immediately
commenced his school.   Soon after he obtained a tent
from Fort Ripley, 22 miles distant, in which the school
was continued until the autumn, when the first log building was completed.   To this additions were made from
year to year, until the St. Columba Mission House was
the result, with its church and bell.

The work of teaching soon demanded more laborers,
and teachers came from the East.   Mr. Samuel Hall,
Miss Mills, who afterwards became Mrs. Breck; Miss
Frink, Miss West, Miss Allen and Miss Wells were
among the assistants from time to time.   Charles Selkrig
and Enmegabowh acted as interpreters, and Mr. John
Parker, now of St. Paul, was employed in the erection
of the buildings from 1852 to 1857.

Northward from Gull Lake, about 60 miles, is Leech
Lake, the home of the Ojibwa band called "The Pillagers."
Their name seems to have been quite a good index to
their character, in those years.   In 1838 they had, by
their annoyances, driven away Rev. T. W. Boutwell and
wife, missionaries of the American Board; and in like
manner, in the year 1845, they made it impossible for missionaries of the American Missionary Association to remain.   But now, in the year 1856, these same wild Pillagers
by their head man, invite Rev. Mr. Breck to establish a
school at Leech Lake. and give him control of their edu-

cational money. Will they do better by him than they did by former missionaries? We shall see.

Buildings were erected at Leech Lake, near the head of the Mississippi, in the summer of 1856, and on the 12th of November of that year, Mr. Breck, with his family and assistants, removed to the new mission. On the same day that Mr. Breck left Gull Lake, Rev. E. S. Peake arrived to take charge of the St. Columba Mission. Mr. Peake was a young clergyman from the Nashotah seminary, who had spent the previous year in frontier work in the valley of the Minnesota and in the Sioux country, and was appointed to the mission among the Ojibwas by Rt. Rev. Bishop Jackson Kemper, then the Bishop in charge of Minnesota. Mr. Peake went with his wife in the stage from St. Paul to Gull lake.

Mr. Charles W. Rees and his family, with Miss Emily West and Miss Kate Heron, spent the winter at Leech Lake, with Mr. and Mrs. Breck.

In the spring of 1857, the turbulent spirits among the Pillagers became very insolent and troublesome, partly, at least, in consequence of the removal of the U. S. troops from Fort Ripley. Mr. Breck's life was repeatedly threat-ened by Indians, who came to the Mission House, breaking the windows with clubs, and entering the house in their war dress of paint and feathers. This conduct forced Mr. Breck to retire from Leech Lake, and abandon the mission there, which he did in June, 1857, after residing there only eight months.

The same causes which forced the abandonment of the upper mission in June, soon led to violence in the vicinity of St. Columba. The murder of a German by some intoxicated young Indians, was followed by the arrest of three, who were summarily executed by lynch law, on their way to St. Paul for trial. This greatly exasperated the Indians, and endangered the lives of the missionaries. Mr. Peake with his wife and sister, and Miss Frink and Charles Selkrig retired, for a time, to Fort Ripley, which was in charge of an ordnance Sergeant and the Chaplain. Enmegahbowh remained at the mission. The troops were soon ordered back to Fort Ripley, but the commanding officer considered it unsafe for the members of the Mission to spend the winter among the Indians, and invited the missionary to occupy a set of vacant officers' quarters in the garrison. This he thankfully accepted. Fifteen children were brought from the Mission, and the school was kept up, while Mr. Peake continued to visit St. Columba, 22 miles distant, at the end of each week, for divine service, performing the journey usually on foot.

In the spring of 1858, the Mission family returned to St. Columba; and in the summer of that year, John Johnson —Enmegahbowh—was admitted by Bishop Kemper to the first order of the Episcopal ministry, at Faribault.

Rev. James L. Breck, on retiring from the Indian country, established Mission schools at Faribault, one of which was for Indian children, named after the first missionary to the Mohawks, Andrews Hall. It was in the care of Miss Susan L. Phelps, Miss Mary J. Mills and Miss Emily J. West. It had from twenty to thirty Indian children of Ojibwa and Sioux parentage. "Of these children," Bishop Whipple writes afterwards: "Several have become ministers of Jesus Christ."

In the summer of 1859, Mr. Peake removed with his family across the Mississippi to Crow Wing, in the edge of the reservation, and built a chapel there, Rev. John Johnson continuing in charge at Gull Lake, and Mr. Peake still had a general supervision, and visited St. Columba every month to celebrate the holy communion. This continued for three years until the Sioux outbreak in 1862, when the St. Columba Mission was broken up by the war parties. John Johnson alone remained and continued to preach the gospel to his people as a forlorn hope, encouraged by the chaplain at Fort Ripley and by Bishop Whipple, who was now in charge of the diocese of Minnesota.

In the year of our Lord, 1859, the Right Rev. H. B. Whipple was consecrated Bishop of the Protestant Episcopal church of Minnesota. It is the testimony of others, that from his first coming into the country, he took a deep interest in the salvation of the red men, visiting the country every year, and traversing it from Crow Wing to Red Lake in canoe and on foot, that he might preach the coming of the Son of God in all their villages. How he has stood up manfully and Christianly, and plead the cause of the Indian, in the face of opposition and scorn, in high places and low places, many of us know right well.

At the time of his coming, and for years after, hope for the salvation of the Ojibwa Indians had well nigh died out. The picture drawn by the Bishop is a very dark one, as well as a true one. At that time, the Rev. J. Lloyd Breck had been driven from the Mission at Leech Lake, by drunken Indians. The Rev. E. S. Peake had been compelled to remove his family from Gull Lake to Crow Wing. The missionaries of the American Board had retired from this part of field some years before. The Methodist Mission at Sandy Lake and the Mission at Rabbit Lake were things of the past. And in this year, 1859, the American Missionary Association, owing to annoyances and exactions of drunken Indians, had withdrawn their Missions from Red Lake and Lake Winnebegoshish. Thus Christian work for the Ojibwas seemed hopeless. The deadly fire-water flowed freely—vice and immorality were open and unblushing. The poor Indians were dragged down to depths of degradation their fathers never knew. Only one clergyman, Rev. John Johnson, Enmegahbowh, remained among the Ojibwas.

The Mission at Gull Lake was destroyed by the Indians during the outbreak of 1862. Rev. E. S. Peake became a chaplain in the army in 1863. For several years there did not seem to be a ray of light on their future. Each year Bishop Whipple, with John Johnson and others of his clergy, traveled hundreds of miles in the Indian country, to tell the story of God's love. They saw but little fruit of their labors.

But in 1869, a new era commenced. A few Indians were induced to remove to a new reservation at White Earth. Others followed until all of the Gull Lake band, as well as many others, were removed. For the first time this people had an abiding place—a home. Rev. John Johnson removed with his people, and commenced services in a log house. Some of the chiefs and head men were converted; among these, one of the great warriors of the tribe, named Nabonaskong. His whole soul was consecrated to the new service. He talked constantly of the love of Jesus Christ, and with tears plead with his heathen countrymen to turn to God. Many were baptised, and a church and parsonage were built.

In 1874, Rev. Joseph A. Gilfillan joined the Mission, and a school was opened for the training of Indian clergy. A Mission house, and also a hospital with thirty beds, were erected. Since then *eight* Indians have been ordained to the ministry: Samuel Madison, Frederick Smith, George Johnson, Charles Wright, John Coleman, George Smith, Mark Hart and George B. Morgan. And Rev. Edwin Bene· dict, · an Indian clergyman from Canada has joined the Mission.

When, in the first term of Gen. Grant's administration, the arrangement was made to divide up the Indian field, and give to the various religious denominations the nomination of Indian agents, the whole of the Ojibwa nation was assigned to the American Missionary Association. Thus, this Association selected the agents for Lake Superior and Leech Lake and Red Lake and White Earth agencies. They also selected and sent out teachers, whose salaries were paid out of government funds. This was the case at Leech Lake. At Red Lake the A. M. A., for a number of years, supported a missionary, Rev. Francis- Spees. This was their second occupation of this field; the first having been given up in 1859. The writer of this paper visited Leech Lake and Red Lake in the summer of 1874, in connection with other agencies, and to him the whole Ojibwa country appeared like an open and promising field.

But for reasons satisfactory to themselves, mainly it is believed financial, the Congregational church relinquished their Mission at Red Lake in 1877, and in 1879, their school at Leech Lake, and both places have been occupied by Bishop Whipple. Church buildings have been erected at the agency at Red Lake, at Mah-dwa-go-nind's village on Red Lake; at Wild Rice River, at Leech Lake and at Pembina settlement. The plan of the Bishop is to send out his Indian clergy two and two. All of the above churches are in the charge of Indian clergymen, whose devotion and piety will compare favorably with that of their white brothers.

Last fall the Indians at White Earth held their first agricultural fair. There were fifteen hundred and twenty entries, representing twenty-five thousand bushels of wheat, besides large quantities of other cereals, and every variety of vegetables and household industry. The exhibitors were Iudians, the judges were Indians and the police were Indians. U. S. Senator McMillan said that the fair would compare favorably with any county fair he had ever attended. The Indians at White Earth are a civilized people, as quiet and orderly as any in the state. And there is a marked movement going on throughout the whole Ojibwa nation, leading them to Christian civilization.

Bishop Whipple has confirmed 350 Ojibwas. And the Episcopal church has at this time *one* hundred christian families of five hundred souls, and about 250 communicants. This has been accomplished without government to punish crime, without law to protect the innocent, without individual titles to property, but is the result of the gospel of Jesus Christ.

Almost half a century has passed since the first missionaries of the American Board entered this part of the Ojibwa field. Then came the Methodist missionaries in 1839. Four years after this, in 1843, the American Missionary Association sent in a large force, and occupied several stations. Then in 1852, the Protestant Episcopal church commenced Mission work. True and earnest hearted workers, men and women, lived and labored many years among the Ojibwas for this uplifting, and some died on the field. Among thorns, on stony places, and on the hard beaten roads of sin, they scattered the seeds of life. At length these seeds, though buried long, have sprung up and grown and fruited. To Bishop Whipple, in the main, it has been granted to gather the harvest. And we all thank God for it. Thus it is still true, that one soweth and another reapeth. But blessed shall be both the sowers and the reapers, for they shall rejoice together, in the spiritual harvest.

The Episcopal Mission among the Sioux was commenced by Bishop Whipple in 1860. This was at what was called Red Wood or Lower Sioux Agency. The missionaries of the American Board had a small number of church members at this place. These were mainly those who had been members of Dr. Williamson's church at Raponia, before their removal. Rev. John P. Williamson had just finished his Seminary course at Lane Seminary, and was to come out and occupy the Lower Agency in this autumn of 1860. Bishop Whipple was doubtless not fully acquainted with these facts, when he acted on the request of the chiefs of the Lower Sioux Agency, to establish a Mission among them. At the time, the Presbyterian missionaries felt that he hardly acted towards them in accordance with the principles of Missionary comity; but they have since been abundantly satisfied that the movement was of the Lord, that thereby the good Bishop might be identified with the spiritual work for the Sioux against the time of need.

In the autumn of 1860, he sent Rev. Samuel D. Hinman and wife and Miss Emily J. West to this Agency, when a Mission and school were commenced with every promise of success. A small Christian company had been gathered, when the Mission was destroyed by the outbreak of August, 1862. Every Christian Indian was faithful during this terrible war. The lives of the white captives were saved by the members of the Presbyterian and Episcopal churches. They rescued more than a hundred women and children from captivity. The story of their heroism reads like the tales of the early church. Taopi, Good Thunder, Owancha-maza, like John Other Day, Simon Anawangmane, Paul Mazakootamane and Lorenzo Lawrence performed deeds of bravery which deserved the gratitude of the whole American people.

The Episcopal Mission was continued in the camp of Indian prisoners at Fort Snelling, and removed with the Indians to Crow Creek on the Missouri river. Bishop Whipple confirmed one hundred and thirty-seven Sioux while the Mission was under his care. In 1875 he licensed George W. St. Clair, a Sioux Indian as catechist and lay reader, to care for the scattered families of Sioux residing at Faribault, Shakopee, Mendota and Red Wing. He was ordained in 1879, and is now an itinerant missionary to his people. About thirty persons, in these settlements, have been confirmed.

SECTION IX.

MISSION OF THE AMERICAN BOARD AMONG THE SIOUX OR DAKOTAS, CONTINUED—1853.

It will be remembered that, as a result of the Treaties of 1851, the Sioux were removed from the Mississippi and Lower Minnesota, to reservations on the Red Wood and Yellow Medicine, and that consequently the Stations at Red Wing, Little Crow's Village, Oak Grove, Prairie-ville and Traverse des Sioux were abandoned, all the missionaries connected with these Stations, except Dr. Williamson, electing to remain and labor among the white people. It was also noted that Dr. Williamson had, in the autumn of 1852, occupied a new Station a few miles above the Yellow Medicine. Also that in the next year Mr. Adams had received a call to take charge of the Church at Traverse des Sioux, which he had accepted. Mr. and Mrs. Pettijohn had also left Lac qui Parle and taken a homestead in the neighborhood of Traverse des Sioux, so that there were but the two families left, Dr. Williamson's and my own. Jane P. Williamson resided with her brother at Pay-zhe-hoo-ta-zee, and taught the school; while in my own family, we were fortunate to have Miss Lucy Spooner, afterwards Mrs. Drake, for two years after our return in the summer of 1852. Thus the work was carried on at the Yellow Medicine and Lac qui Parle. At the latter place, on the 3d of March, 1854, our Mission buildings took fire and were burned to ashes, including almost their entire contents. This event brought out largely the sympathy of our Dakota friends and others, near and far off.

After this event, and while we were preparing to re-build at Lao qui Parle, Rev. S. B. Treat, of Boston, visited our Mission, and, after due consideration, it was decided that our strength was now in a greater consolidation. We were only two families, and it was wisely judged that we could be more helpful to each other, as well as carry on the Mission work to greater advantage, if we were nearer together. The annuities would now be paid at the Yellow Medicine, and our Christian Indians were quite willing to begin anew nearer to the Agency, and so in the summer of 1854, we built within two miles of Dr. Williamson, calling our station, at first, New Hope, but afterwards changing it to Hazelwood.

The plan was now, to commence a boarding school at the new station, as soon as possible, and to gather around the two stations as many as were willing to come under the arrangements of a civilized and Christianized community. This plan was eminently successful. To meet the requirements for building, a circular saw mill was put in operation by the Mission. This furnished the lumber to put up a building, the next year (1855), for the boarding school, and also a neat chapel. Of the $700 required for this last object, $500 was raised by the Indians and their white friends. Also, in the course of a few years, the Dakota and half blood families were helped to good frame buildings. The government soon commenced to erect for them dwellings of brick. The community here was soon organized into a civilized band called the Hazelwood Republic, and was the pattern for the government at the Lower Sioux Agency. The boarding school went into operation early in 1856, conducted for the first two years or more, by Miss Ruth Pettijohn and Mrs. Anna B. Ackley. In 1859, Mr. Hugh D. Cunningham became steward of the boarding school, and continued in this position until the outbreak of 1862. It accommodated from sixteen to twenty scholars. Besides Mrs. Ackley, Misses Eliza W. Huggins and Isabella B. Riggs, were at different times employed as teachers.

In the early spring of 1857, occurred the Spirit Lake massacre, which proved a disturbing element in our Mission work during the whole summer. Of the four female captives taken by Inkpa-doota's party, two perished and two were brought in by Indians who had learned humanity from the Bible. Agent Flandrau found efficient help in executing summary justice upon one of Inkpa-doota's sons, who had the temerity to come into the Yellow Medicine settlement during that summer. Of the disturbances and dangers of the season, Dr. Williamson, in the November following, wrote a very full and graphic account, which was published in the *Missionary Herald* for February, 1858. It may said that all these things turned out for the furtherance of the gospel. Year by year some additions were made to each of the churches, so that our aggregate membership was now more than sixty. Since this new departure we had a new Dakota hymn book prepared with the tunes. Also, the first part of Bunyan's Pilgrim's Progress, which I had translated into Dakota, was printed and became an inspiration to our people.

At St. Paul, on September 8, 1858, the Synod of Minnesota was organized, consisting of the Presbyterians of Dakota, Minnesota and Blue Earth. Dr. Williamson, as the oldest minister, preached the sermon, in which he gave

—10

a minute account of the trials, toils and sacrifices, as well
as encouragements, attendant on planting the gospel
among the Dakotas.   But I refer to this organization of
the synod (which will have its proper place in a paper
by another hand), simply to say, that of the twenty-one
ministers which constituted it, exactly one-third had been,
or were, missionaries among the Sioux.

The Indians, who removed from the Mississippi, located
at the Red Wood or Lower Sioux Agency.   Of them, eight
or ten persons had been members of the Kaposia and Oak
Grove churches.   These were counted as a part of Dr.
Williamson's church, and in 1861, were organized separ-
ately.   In the spring of 1860, John P. Williamson, the
Doctor's eldest son, finished his theological studies at Lane
Seminary, and, after preaching a few months in Indiana,
came and took charge of this little church at the Lower
Sioux Agency.   The next summer he erected a nice little
frame chapel, which was dedicated in the last days of the
year 1861.   Before he had completed his dwelling house,
the outbreak of August, 1862, came on, when Mr. William
son was providentially absent on a visit to Ohio.

The causes of this outbreak were not difficult to see.
The Republican administration, as it came in, managed
matters unwisely in several particulars—notably in an attempt to change the money annuities into goods, and in
the consequent failure to meet their engagements at the
proper time in the summer of 1862.   By this course of
the government, as well as by a knowledge of the defeats
of our armies in the Southern war, the Sioux of the Minnesota were kept in a state of dissatisfaction and unrest,
ever since the autumn of 1861.   At the Lower Sioux

Agency a *Tee–go–tee–pee*, or Soldier's Lodge, was organized, which always had been done, either for the protection of the Buffalo hunt or for war. This was the evidence of their disaffection and excitement. Lying still deeper than the causes before mentioned was an extensive opposition to the adoption of the forms of civilization which had been pressed upon them. The administration had held out strong inducements to Indian men to have their hair cut off and adopt a civilized dress; and this had been attended by a large measure of success. This, to the so-called medicine men, represented a change of religion, and, naturally enough, provoked a strong opposition.

The outbreak itself, with its horrors and devastation, with its deaths and deliverances, may be mainly passed over, as not germane to the object of this paper. But the world has a right to know what part our Christian Indians took in this emeute. Bishop Whipple testifies: "Every Christian Indian was faithful during this terrible war. The lives of the white captives were saved by the members of the Presbyterian and Episcopal churches. They rescued more than one hundred women and children from captivity. The story of their heroism reads like the tales of the early church." Let us see how far this statement is true. Taopi, Good Thunder, Owanca-maza and others breasted the storm of the outbreak at the Lower Sioux Agency. The next morning, John Otherday, started with the company of white people, sixty-two in numbers, from the Yellow Medicine and brought them safely to St. Paul. Our missionary company of forty odd persons, were materially assisted in making our escape by more than a dozen of our Christian men. Peter–Big–Fire went with a war party, which was likely to follow *our trail*, until they had passed over it, and then returned, having accomplished his object. While Gen. Sibley's force still lay at Fort Ridgely, Lorenzo Lawrence brought down two canoe loads in one of which was Mrs. DeCamp and her children. About the same time, Simon Anawangmane brought to our camp, in his one-horse wagon, Mrs. Newman and her children. In the meantime, Paul Mazakootamane, backed by John B. Renville and his noble wife and others, worked in the hostile camp, to bring about a counter revolution, got into their possession the white captives, and were ready to deliver them up, after the battle of Wood Lake. This was done at Camp Release. These were all prominent men in our Mission churches. Surely Christianity is sufficiently vindicated. True, Peter–Big–Fire and Robert Hopkins, and one or two other members of our churches, were condemned and imprisoned, *because they had carried their guns* and had *been present at some of the battles.* But this imprisonment, like the Apostle Paul's at Cæsarea, and at Rome, was for the furtherance of the gospel.

SECTION X.

MISSION OF THE AMERICAN BOARD WITH THE OJIBWAS, 1854 TO 1880.

The attempt to establish the government school at Crow Wing having proved a failure, and Rev. Thomas Hall having retired to Sauk Rapids where he made himself a home, Mr. Pulsifer and his wife with Henry Blatchford, native catechist, returned to Lake Superior and were thenceforward a part of the Mission at Red River with Mr. and Mrs. Wheeler. This was now the only station of the American Board with the Ojibwas. The government at Washington had now become satisfied of the bad policy of attempting to remove the Lake Superior Indians to the interior of Minnesota, and had abandoned it. In the fall of 1853 a payment had been made on the lake, and now in the autumn of 1854, a commission, consisting of Agents Gilbert and Harriman, was authorized to treat with those Ojibwas on and near the lake in Minnesota and Wisconsin for a cession of their land. This treaty was made and ratified, and was regarded as fair and honorable to both parties — six reservations being allotted to the Indians, one of which was on Bad River. By this treaty it was arranged that the Indians could secure in severalty eighty acres of land for a homestead. This proved quite an incentive to industry, and in the course of a few years many of these Indians had built cabins and made homes for themselves on their eighty acre lots. The *metawa*, their sacred dance, was allowed to go into disuse; their children attended the Mission school, and many of the principal families ranged themselves on the side of the "praying Indians," and pretty much the whole band exerted themselves to keep whisky away from the reserve. A half-breed who was known to be a liquor seller, applied for permission to come and be their teacher. The chief men said, "No; it is true we like a drop once in a while ourselves, but we are afraid to have whisky come here among our people." That was a brave stand to take.

In addition to the workers mentioned above, Miss Spooner was there as the school teacher. The school prospered, having an average attendance of thirty scholars. A school at La Pointe was also maintained for a part of the time, as Indians still resided there for the purpose of fishing. The hearers of the Word were more numerous than heretofore; and a few showed an honest desire to obey the gospel. This appears to have been the condition of Mission work at this station for several years — that of slow but manifest progress in the line of civilization and evangelization. In the summer of 1856, Secretary S. B. Treat from Boston visited this mission, when the plan was adopted for the establishment of a mission boarding school. For the erection of buildings needful to carry out this plan the government of the United States afterwards granted the sum of $3,000. In the report of the board it was noted that D. Irenæus Miner and wife had joined this Mission, "to take charge of the boarding school." In the meantime, Mr. Wheeler places this upon the record: "Many things look like substantial progress among our people. They are much more industrious, temperate and enterprising than formerly. There is evidently a growing desire to own individual property and make homes for themselves and their children. Personal religion, too, is becoming more a matter of independent individual inquiry. And they seem to have, also, more discernment of what spiritual religion is." This was written in the first days of the year 1860.

The boarding school, spoken of above, went into effect in the October preceding with fifteen scholars, which number had been increased to twenty-four a year afterwards, and a large day school was also carried on in connection with the boarding scholars. The steward of the boarding school was David B. Spencer, and Mr. Miner and Miss Rhoda W. Spicer were the teachers, and Henry Blatchford was the native preacher. After the first year or so Mr. Miner and his wife appear to have retired from the Mission.

On March 6, 1862, Mr. Wheeler wrote very encouragingly of the winter's work and of the prospects generally. From 80 to 100 persons had attended their Sabbath services pretty regularly. And they were greatly encouraged by "the best schools they had ever had." Thus at Odanah, which was now the name of the station on Bad River, the work of Education went on prosperously for several years, and the people made "decided progress in the arts and comforts of life." But the church remained in numbers about what it had been. The report of the Board for 1863 says, "no additions; and there is great need of the reviving influences of the Spirit." It must then have been a matter of joy, when Mr. Wheeler could write on the 23d of February, 1864, "The Holy Spirit seems to be present, convincing of sin, especially among the youth in the boarding school and in Christian families."

As the result of this religious awakening, it was believed that "a few were renewed by the Holy Spirit, and the moral condition of the communicants had improved." In 1865, Dr. Ellis took charge of the boarding school, and it is spoken of as continuously doing a good work. But on other accounts the condition of things was far from satisfactory. The Indians became distrustful of the government, and did not feel secure in their homes. This led them to go back somewhat to their *metawa* and other pagan customs. The Indian Department at Washington did not support the boarding school as it should have done. And the spiritual blessing so long hoped for, did not come. And the committee said in their report on this

Mission, "It is painful to learn that the prospects of this tribe are becoming less rather than more hopeful."

In the year following (1866), only Mr. and Mrs. Wheeler and Henry Blatchford are mentioned as occupying the Odanah station; and the report says: "The prospects of the Ojibwa Mission have not improved; and it has become quite obvious that there should be a large reduction in the annual disbursements for its support, if nothing more." Mr. Wheeler's health has not been good for some time, and the next year the family removed to Beloit, Wis., where only a few years of life are added to him. But he had made his mark upon the civilization and Christianization of the Ojibwas of Lake Superior. Henry Blatchford was still retained at Odanah as the native preacher. In the year 1870, this Mission was transferred to the Presbyterian Board.

In the month of September, 1874, it was my privilege to visit this station, as also other agencies among the Ojibwas. The Odanah station was then occupied by Rev. Isaac Baird, assisted by Mrs. Baird, Miss Phillips, Miss Verbeck, Miss Dougherty and Miss Walker. The boarding school had been revived and was in prosperity. I was obliged to confess that I had not seen anywhere, twenty-five boys and girls better looking and more manly and womanly in their appearance, than those Ojibwas. And the whole community gave evidence of the good work done by the school in past years. Since that time, the native church has greatly increased in numbers, and Henry Blatchford has become the native pastor. Finally the government has made arrangements which are supposed to be satisfactory to those Indians in regard to the ownership of land. *The fifty years missionary work has been a success.*

SECTION XI.

MISSION OF THE AMERICAN BOARD AMONG THE SIOUX — CONTINUED — 1862 TO 1880.

The outbreak of August, 1862, came upon us like an avalanche. The day before it commenced, the Mission church at Hazelwood had a grand gathering at the remembrance of the death and resurrection of Christ the Lord. But now it seemed to us as if the very foundations were destroyed, and our work of more than a quarter of a century had come to naught. What could be the moral meaning of the events, and what would be its results, we could not tell. During the days and nights spent on the prairie in making our escape these questions often came up; but the whole was an enigma — dark, doubtful.

Step by step the way was made plain. The first thing to be done was the delivery of the white captives. The next was to see that justice should be done in punishing the guilty and shielding the innocent. Then there opened up a work in the prison at Mankato and in the camp at Fort Snelling that we little dreamed of. In both places during winter there grew up an enthusiasm for education and a hunger for hearing the words of life. Rev. John P. Williamson returned from Ohio immediately on hearing of the outbreak, joined our camp at Red Wood, went with the Indian families — about 1,500 persons — in their journey to Snelling, and thence in the next spring to Crow Creek, and was their spiritual Moses during all the years of their separation and affliction. Dr. Williamson, locating his family at Saint

Peter, was ready to enter the open door of the prison at Mankato. The opposition to education, and the gospel of Christ, had vanished. The prison became a school of letters and religion, and the camp at Fort Snelling was not much behind. In midwinter Dr. Williamson summoned to his aid Rev. G. H. Pond, and they two baptised 300 prisoners in one day. At the camp John P. Williamson was indefatiguable in his labors, and more than 100 hopeful conversions took place. Many adults and children were baptised. It was my privi. lege to work somewhat at both places, and to witness the marvels which God was working in their dark minds and hearts.

It is matter of history that the condemned men were taken in the spring of 1863 to Camp McClellan at Davenport, Iowa, where they were kept for three years. The families of these men were taken around by the mouth of the Missouri and landed at Fort Thompson or Crow Creek, in Dakota. Something more than a score of Dakota men were selected by Gen. Sibley as scouts, and they and their families were retained in Minnesota.

By the removals of the inmates of the prison and the camp, the main part of our Mission work among the Sioux was removed beyond the range of this paper. But I cannot forbear saying that the educational and religious work went on in both communities. Of the three winters that followed, Dr. Williamson spent two, and I spent one with the prisoners at Davenport. While J. P. Williamson, summoning to his aid Edward R. Pond and H. D. Cunningham, for a part of the time cared for the intellectual and spiritual wants of the women and children at Crow Creek. These were years of great mortality. At least one-tenth died every year. But when, in the summer of 1866, the *reunion* of the families took place at Niobrara, in the north east corner of Nebraska, the consolidated church numbered over 400. So had the word of God taken root among them. In the meantime it had been a part of my duty and privilege to revise and complete the translation of the entire New Testament into the language of the Dakotas, which, together with a revised Genesis and Proverbs, by Dr. Williamson, was printed for us by the American Bible Society, in the first days of 1865. This met a great and increasing want among these Christian Sioux. In the summer that followed, more than $100 were paid by the imprisoned men at Davenport, for Dakota Bibles.

After Gen. Sibley's campaign of 1863, the Sioux men who had been employed as scouts on the expedition, joined their families, and were stationed on the frontier as a guard against the incursions of the hostiles. For several years they were retained under the direction of the military, and formed what we called the Scouts' camp. Among them a church was organized. With John B. Renville, who for some years after the outbreak resided in St. Anthony, I visited this camp in the summer of 1864, at the Yellow Medicine, and in 1865, at the head of the Red Wood. When Mr. Renville was licensed and ordained as an Evangelist, he was for some time in special charge of this scattered flock. A part of them stopped at Lac qui Parle and made claims. But when in the summer of 1866, Dr. Williamson and myself, taking with us Mr. Renville, went on a tour of visitation, we found the majority of the scouts encamped on the shores of Lake Traverse and at Buffalo Lake, within the limits of this present reserve.

We had now reached that point in our Mission work where it became necessary to employ native helpers, more than we had hitherto done. John B. Renville had been licensed the year before by the Dakota Presbytery meeting at Mankato. This summer of 1866, we approbated four other men to preach the gospel among their people—two on the Couteau and two on the Missouri. This work of inducting Dakota men into the office of the ministry was continued from year to year, as our Christian communities demanded. Putting the work mainly upon others, Dr. Williamson and I spent our summers in the field and our winters at our homes in St. Peter and Beloit, in carrying forward the translation of the Bible, and in doing other needed work.

In 1867, those Indians made a treaty with the government, by which the present reservation was set apart for their occupation, and a promise made them of help in their efforts to become civilized. From that time they began to scatter and settle down in various parts of the reserve. Each summer we held a camp meeting with them, when new members were added to the church rolls. In the summer of 1868, the number added on profession of faith was more than three-score. Indians came on to the reserve from the Missouri, from the north and from the white settlements. Thus the community in a few years numbered a thousand—then 1500 and more. It was now necessary to organize them into separate churches. The first of these to have native pastors were the Ascension and Long Hollow churches, which were in charge of Rev. J. B. Renville and Rev. Solomon Toonkanshaecheya. The other Dakota churches in this region were Lac qui Parle, Dry Wood Lake and Kettle Lakes. The latter was with the scouts in Fort Wadsworth. We had several licentiates, as Daniel Renville, Peter, Simon and Louis.

In the summer of 1870, I erected Mission buildings on this reserve near the agency, which station we called Good Will. This gave to our occupation more of permanence, and it became the center of our work for that part of the country. The two winters following I spent there myself, but the Mission school was placed in charge of Mr. W. K. Morris. In 1872, Rev. M. N. Adams became agent, and during nearly four years pushed forward the work of education, erecting several district school houses, and one large building for a boarding school. In all the years since that time, this boarding school has been in operation, and has done good work. Under every agent from Dr. J. W. Daniels to the present one, Charles Crissey, civilization has progressed on this reservation. Under the exceedingly difficult arrangements of the treaty of 1867, a few individuals have obtained patents for the land they occupy. All are anxious to become land owners. This was very strongly manifested by two colonies going off from the reservations and taking homesteads. The first company went out from the Santee agency a dozen years ago, and commenced the homestead settlement at Flandrau on the Big Sioux, a few miles west of the Minnesota line. Now it numbers about four-score families, and is a prosperous settlement, with both a Presbyterian and an Episcopal church. The other colony went from the Sisseton reserve about six years ago. It consists of about thirty families, who have, largely of their own resources, built a good house of worship, and have a church of seventy members. Thus it has become apparent that Indians are capable of becoming civilized and Christianized, and thus pass from the anomolous position of dependence into that of citizenship. We claim that the Indian problem is being worked out. That the Bible is the great civilizer of the nations—Indians as well as others.

The present number of native churches on this Sisseton reservation, including the Brown Earth homestead settlement, is six, with an aggregate membership of about 400. Another step in the religious progress of this people is indexed by the existence of a Native Missionary Society, which raises and uses in employing missionaries to the wilder Sioux, between three and four hundred dollars annually. The Ascension church—Rev. John B. Renville, pastor, has a house of worship which cost them about $1500. Mayasan church, at the other end of the reserve, has a house which cost about $500. Long Hollow church has a log-house which is comfortable if not attractive. Buffalo Lake and Good Will churches have buildings in process of erection.

Three years ago the Missionary Society of Canada called one of our native pastors, Rev. Solomon Toonkansharcheya, to do Mission work among the dispersed Sioux in Manitoba, which is proving a successful undertaking. Thus with the whole Bible in the language of the Sioux, and with churches and native pastors in working order, I may close this paper by recognizing the divine hand and the divine help in all the forty odd years of our Mission work among the Sioux. Dr. T. S. Williamson, the father of our Mission, has gone to the upper world; and so has the younger of the brothers

Pond. But both lived to see the gospel working out the uplift of the Dakotas beyond their highest anticipations. It is indeed marvelous in our eyes.

Beloit, Wis., May 1880.

MEMOIR OF REV. STEPHEN R. RIGGS, D. D.

[This issue of our collections, being the first one published since the death of Dr. Riggs, makes it proper to give a brief memoir of this devoted missionary, in connection with his valuable paper, as above.]

Stephen Return Riggs, was the descendant of Miles Riggs, a native of Wales, who settled in Plymouth, Mass., soon after the arrival of the first pilgrims. His parents were Stephen Riggs and Annie Baird. He was born in Steubenville, O., March 12, 1812., one of eleven children. In 1829, the family removed to Ripley, O., where, in the August following, his mother died. Sixteen years later his father died. Stephen Riggs commenced his academic education in Ripley, and in the spring of 1833, went to Jefferson College, Pa., where he was graduated in 1834. He studied theology partly at the Western Theological Seminary at Allegheny, Pa., and was licensed to preach by the Chillicothe Presbytery, in the autumn of 1836. The following winter he spent in Hawley, Mass., and preached to the West Parish people. During the winter, he was accepted by the Prudential Committee of the American Board as a missionary, and designated to join the Dakota Mission. Returning to Ohio in the spring, he was ordained as a missionary to the Dakotas, by the Chillicothe Presbytery, at West Union, O., in April, 1837. On Feb. 16, 1837, he was married to Miss Mary Ann Clark Longley, in Hawley, Mass., an estimable and devoted woman, who bravely bore all the hardships and dangers of missionary life, for over quarter of a century. They started for their field of work in March, and reached the Lake Harriet Mission, near the Falls of St. Anthony, in June, 1837, where Dr. Riggs began his life-long labors for the Dakota Indians, going to Lac qui Parle in September of the same year. Dr. Williamson and the Pond brothers had already begun the work in this region. He gave diligent study to the Dakota tongue, soon speaking it with fluency, and translating the scriptures, hymns, and other works into it; besides laboring faithfully for the spiritual and temporal welfare of the natives. In 1840, he made a journey to Ft. Pierre. In 1842, while on a visit east, he supervised the printing of a considerable portion of the Bible, in Dakota, also a hymn book and some school books, of which he had performed most of the authorship. In the spring of 1843, he returned to his mission field, and established a new station at Traverse de Sioux, but in 1846 was sent again to Lac qui Parle, where he continued to labor until 1854, in the meantime spending a winter (1851–52) east, supervising the printing of the "Grammar and Dictionary of the Dakota Language," compiled by himself and his associates in the mission work, Dr. Thomas S. Williamson and Revs. Gideon H. and Samuel W. Pond, after many years of patient labor and study. This great work, one of the most important contributions to Indian philology produced in America, owed its publication largely to a fund contributed by members of the Minnesota Historical Society.

On March 3, 1854, the Mission houses at Lac qui Parle were consumed by fire, and they were compelled to remove to Hazel Wood or "Oomahoo," where he resided until the massacre, Aug. 18, 1862, when he and his family were in great danger, but providentially escaped to a place of safety. During the winter of 1862-63, Dr. Riggs labored hard for the conversion of the Indian prisoners confined at Mankato and elsewhere. In the Sibley expedition of 1863 to the Missouri, he served as chaplain and interpreter. He continued his missionary work after the termination of the Indian war, visiting in the summers, Missions in Nebraska and Dakota, and meantime working during winters on his translation of the Bible into Dakota, which was completed and published just before his death, in 1883. He lived during these latter years at Beloit, Wis., in which city Mrs. Mary Riggs, his devoted wife, died.

Dr. Riggs was subsequently remarried. The end of his long and eventful career came to him at Beloit, Aug. 24, 1883, in his 71st year. Dr. Riggs was a man of small stature, but of much endurance and courage. Many times during his stay on the frontier, his life was in danger, but he always faced peril with calmness. He was an industrious scholar, and an observant author. His works are numerous, and all evince ability. The degree of D. D. was conferred upon him in 1873 by Beloit College, and of LL. D., by Jefferson College. An interesting account of his long and faithful labors is given in his work, "Mary and I," published in 1880. Eight children had been born to them, several of whom also engaged in the missionary work among the Dakotas.   W.